My Dear Nuakuluapik

Nunavummi

The Nunavummi reading series is a Nunavut-developed levelled book series that supports literacy development while teaching readers about the people, traditions, and environment of the Canadian Arctic.

Published in Canada by Nunavummi, an imprint of Inhabit Education Books Inc. | www.inhabiteducationbooks.com

Inhabit Education Books Inc.
(Iqaluit) P.O. Box 2129, Iqaluit, Nunavut, X0A 1H0
(Toronto) 614 Mount Pleasant Road, Unit 1, Toronto, Ontario, M4S 2M8

Design and layout copyright © 2022 Inhabit Education Books Inc.
Text copyright © 2022 Irene Jonas
Illustrations by Tindur Peturs © 2022 Inhabit Education Books Inc.

Printed in Canada.

Library and Archives Canada Cataloguing in Publication

Title: My dear Nuakuluapik / written by Irene Jonas ; illustrated by Tindur Peturs.
Names: Jonas, Irene (Children's author), author. | Peturs, Tindur, illustrator.
Series: Nunavummi reading series.
Description: Series statement: Nunavummi reading series
Identifiers: Canadiana 20220280711 | ISBN 9781774505700 (softcover)
Subjects: LCSH: Jonas, Irene (Children's author)—Family—Juvenile fiction. | LCSH: Intergenerational
  relations—Juvenile fiction. | LCGFT: Picture books.
Classification: LCC PS8619.O518 M9 2022 | DDC jC813/.6—dc23

ISBN: 978-1-77450-570-0

INHABIT EDUCATION BOOKS

My Dear Nuakuluapik

WRITTEN BY

Irene Jonas

ILLUSTRATED BY

Tindur Peturs

Nuakuluapik is my mother's mother. When I was born, she named me after her late aunt. I call her Nuakuluapik, which means "my dear aunt."

When my mother and
father went to work,
I would stay with
Nuakuluapik all day.

4

When Nuakuluapik was sewing a parka, she would let me help her.

Nuakuluapik would let me help her take threads off a zipper from an old jacket. Then she used the zipper on the parka she was making.

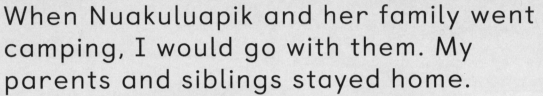

When Nuakuluapik and her family went camping, I would go with them. My parents and siblings stayed home.

I would not get homesick while I was with Nuakuluapik. It was so much fun.

I did not bring toys on the camping trips. Nuakuluapik made me toys from old things.

Today, I am thankful to Nuakuluapik for looking after me. She was a mother, grandmother, and older sister to me.

Nuakuluapik is no longer with us. She is in our hearts and memories. I love Nuakuluapik and miss her very much.

About the Author

Irene Jonas and her husband live in Clyde River with their two children, Audrey and Troy. Irene graduated from the Nunavut Teacher Education Program through Nunavut Arctic College.

About the Illustrator

Tindur Peturs is an animator and illustrator who was born and raised in Iceland and moved to Canada to study animation and Canadian culture. They have a love of nature, animals, and the power of storytelling.

Inuktitut Glossary

The pronunciation guide in this book is intended to support non-Inuktitut speakers in their reading of Inuktitut words. This pronunciation is not an exact representation of how the word is pronounced by Inuktitut speakers. For more resources on how to pronounce Inuktitut and Inuinnaqtun words, visit inhabiteducation.com/inuitnipingit.

nuakuluapik
noo-AH-koo-loo-ah-pik

my dear aunt

Nunavummi

Nunavummi
Reading Series

The Nunavummi reading series is a Nunavut-developed levelled book series that supports literacy development while teaching readers about the people, traditions, and environment of the Canadian Arctic.

Level 8
- 12-24 pages
- Generally 1–3 sentences per page
- Sentences increase in length and complexity
- Dialogue is introduced in fiction texts, indicated by the word "said"
- Supportive images, but more information now coming from the text

9
- 16-32 pages
- Longer, more complex sentences
- Varied punctuation
- Dialogue is included in fiction texts
- Supportive images, but more information now coming from the text

Level 10
- 16–32 pages
- Sentences and stories become longer and more complex
- Varied punctuation
- Dialogue is included in fiction texts
- Readers rely more on the words than the images to decode the text

Fountas & Pinnell Text Level: I

This book has been officially levelled using the F&P Text Level Gradient™ Leveling System.